WHAT ARE The 5 pillars of Islam?

This book belongs to:

____

24 23 22 21 1 2 3 4

Published by Tughra Books
335 Clifton Ave.
Clifton, NJ, 07011, USA
www.tughrabooks.com

ISBN: 979-8-89729-506-7

Mini Muslims Series ISBN 9781597849692

WHAT ARE The 5 pillars of Islam?

There are 5 things every Muslim must do.

These are called the 5 pillars of Islam.

The first pillar is Shahada.

It is to say: there is no god but Allah

and Muhammad (pbuh) is His messenger.

لَآ اِلٰهَ اِلَّا اللّٰهُ مُحَمَّدٌ رَّسُوْلُ اللّٰهِ

The second pillar is Salah.

It is to pray 5 times a day.

Praying helps us remember Allah.

The third pillar is Zakat.

It is to give money to the needy.

This helps them get food, water,

clothes, a home, and an education.

The fourth pillar is Hajj.

It is to go on a trip to Mecca and join Muslims

from all over the world.

We visit the Kaaba and worship Allah together.

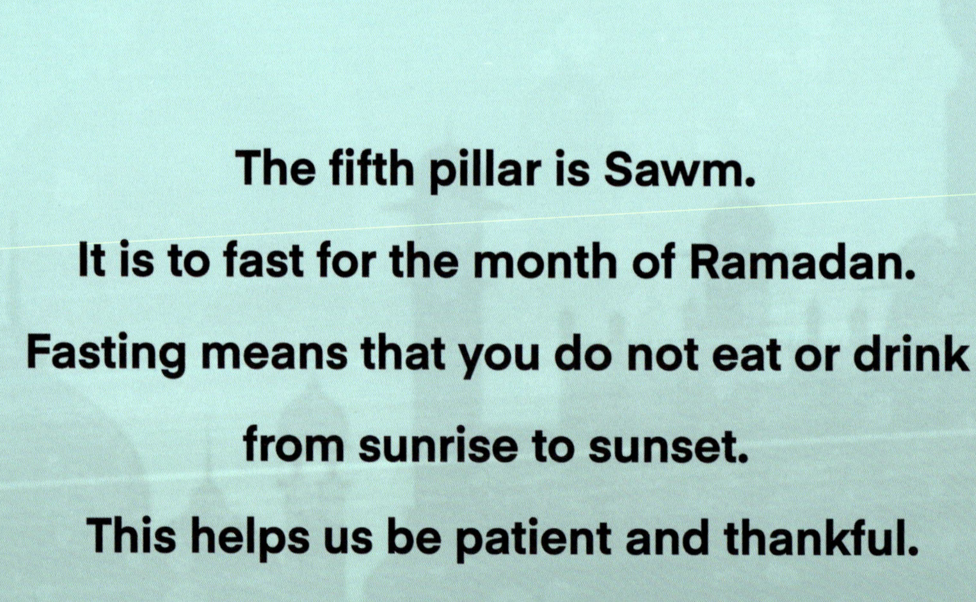

The fifth pillar is Sawm.

It is to fast for the month of Ramadan.

Fasting means that you do not eat or drink

from sunrise to sunset.

This helps us be patient and thankful.